This book belongs to

....

Fireball in the Sky
and Other Stories

How this collection works

This *Biff, Chip and Kipper* collection is one of a series of four books at **Read with Oxford Stage 5**. It contains four stories: *The Ogre's Dinner*, *The Secret Pop Star*, *Fireball in the Sky* and *A Knight in Town*. These stories will help to broaden your child's wider reading experience. There are also fun activities to enjoy throughout the book.

How to use this book

Find a time to read with your child when they are not too tired and are happy to concentrate for about fifteen to twenty minutes, or longer if they are enjoying the story. Reading with your child should be a shared and enjoyable experience. It is best to choose just one of the stories for each session.

For each story, there are tips for reading the story together. At the end of each story you will find four 'Talk about the story' questions. These will help your child to think about what they have read, and to relate the story to their own experiences. The questions are followed by a fun activity.

Enjoy sharing the stories!

Contents

OXFORD
UNIVERSITY PRESS

Authors and illustrators

The Ogre's Dinner written by Paul Shipton, illustrated by Alex Brychta

The Secret Popstar written by Paul Shipton, illustrated by Nick Schon

Fireball in the Sky written by Paul Shipton, illustrated by Nick Schon

A Knight in Town written by Paul Shipton, illustrated by Nick Schon

OXFORD
UNIVERSITY PRESS

Great Clarendon Street, Oxford, OX2 6DP, United Kingdom

Oxford University Press is a department of the University of Oxford. It furthers the University's objective of excellence in research, scholarship, and education by publishing worldwide. Oxford is a registered trade mark of Oxford University Press in the UK and in certain other countries

The Ogre's Dinner, *The Secret Popstar*, *Fireball in the Sky*, *A Knight in Town* text by Paul Shipton © Oxford University Press 2015

The Ogre's Dinner illustrations © Alex Brychta 2015

The Secret Popstar, *Fireball in the Sky*, *A Knight in Town* illustrations by Nick Schon © Oxford University Press 2015

The characters in this work are the original creation of Roderick Hunt and Alex Brychta who retain copyright in the characters

The moral rights of the author have been asserted

The Ogre's Dinner, *The Secret Popstar*, *Fireball in the Sky*, *A Knight in Town* first published in 2015

This Edition first published in 2018

British Library Cataloguing in Publication Data
Data available

ISBN: 978-0-19-276432-4

10 9 8 7 6 5

Paper used in the production of this book is a natural, recyclable product made from wood grown in sustainable forests. The manufacturing process conforms to the environmental regulations of the country of origin.

Printed in China

Acknowledgements

Series Editor: Annemarie Young

Additional artwork by Nick Schon

Tips for reading *The Ogre's Dinner*

Children learn best when reading is relaxed and enjoyable.

- Talk about the title and the picture on page 6. Then read the speech bubble.

- Discuss what you think the story might be about.

- Encourage your child to read as much of the story as they can.

- Give lots of praise as your child reads, and help them when necessary.

- If your child gets stuck on a word that is decodable, encourage them to say the sounds and then blend them together to read the word. Read the whole sentence again. Focus on the meaning.

- If the word is not decodable, or is still too tricky, just read the word for them, re-read the sentence and move on.

- Where you can, use voices for different characters. Encourage your child to do the same. Reading with expression is fun.

- When you've finished reading the story, talk about it with your child, using the 'Talk about the story' questions at the end. Then do the activity.

Children enjoy re-reading stories, and this helps to build their confidence.

Have fun!

For more activities, free eBooks and practical advice to help your child progress with reading visit **oxfordowl.co.uk**

The Ogre's Dinner

Lee was staying at Kipper's house for the night.

"I wonder if the magic key will glow while you're here," said Kipper.

"Me too!" said Lee, who had never been on an adventure.

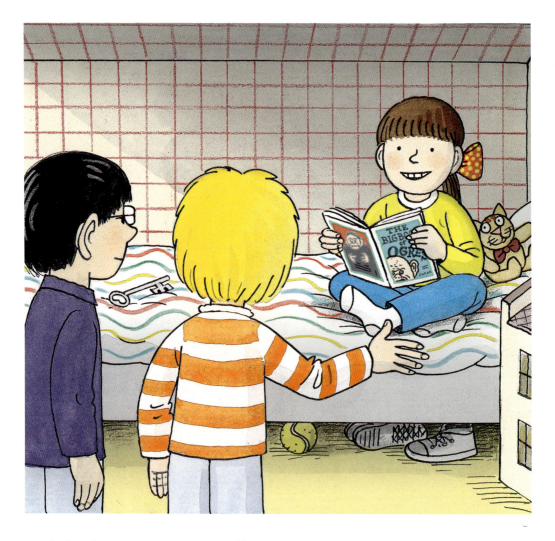

The boys went to Biff's room to check on the key.

"I'll let you know if it starts glowing," Biff told them.

"Do you want to play a board game until then?" Kipper asked her.

"No, thanks," said Biff. "I'm at an exciting bit of my book. The heroes are running away from some hungry ogres."

Lee looked at the book's cover. "What are ogres?" he asked.

"Horrible monsters!" said Biff.

The boys went to Kipper's room. After he put his sleeping bag on the floor, Lee peeked in the wardrobe.

"What are you doing?" asked Kipper.

"Just checking," admitted Lee. "For monsters."

There was the sound of footsteps coming down the hall.

"What's that?" asked Lee. He was a bit jumpy now he had started thinking about monsters.

The door opened.

It was Biff.

"Come quickly," she said. "The key just started glowing!"

Kipper jumped up. Lee followed more slowly, feeling a bit nervous. What if the key took them somewhere scary?

Lee watched Biff pick up the glowing key.

"What happens now?" he asked.

Before Biff or Kipper could answer, the magic began to take them away on an adventure.

The magic took them to a deep, dark forest. A bitter wind howled and made them shiver.

"What now?" Lee asked.

Biff shrugged. "We'll soon find out why the key brought us here."

Suddenly there was a booming noise.

"It's an earthquake!" cried Kipper.

"No," said Biff. "Those are footsteps, and they're getting closer!"

Lee's eyes opened wide. If those were footsteps, some big feet were making them.

A huge head appeared above them.

"A monster!" shouted Lee.

"I am *not* a monster. I'm an ogre!" the ogre sniffed. He looked the children up and down. "And you three look like *strangers*!"

The ogre showed his enormous teeth in a wide grin.

"The King of the Ogres loves strangers," he said. "He'll want to have you for dinner. Follow me." He gestured towards the entrance of a cave.

"Have us for dinner?" thought Lee in alarm. "No, thanks!"

"Run!" shouted Biff.

Lee spun around and followed Biff towards the trees as fast as his legs would take him.

When he finally stopped, Lee's heart was pounding. Biff was by his side, but where was Kipper?

"Oh no! He must have tripped and fallen," said Biff. "We have to go and find him."

They crept back towards the cave, keeping a careful eye out the whole way.

"That ogre was big and scary," said Lee. "I bet the King of the Ogres is even bigger and scarier!"

"Don't worry, Lee," said Biff. "As soon as we've found Kipper, the key will take us home again."

They peeked out just in time to see the ogre disappear
into the cave with Kipper!

"We'll have to go in there to get him," said Biff.

"I don't like this adventure much," said Lee
miserably.

Suddenly two more ogres stomped out of the cave.
The children ducked down as these ogres stomped past.

"Where *are* those children?" asked one ogre. "The
King of the Ogres wants to cook with them."

"*Cook* with us?" whispered Lee. "I don't like the sound of that."

"Me neither!" said Biff crossly. "We're not vegetables, and neither is Kipper! We have to go and rescue him."

Lee and Biff tiptoed to the entrance of the cave.

"Oh no!" groaned Biff. "There are lots of tunnels. How will we ever find Kipper in here?"

Suddenly they heard a shout.

"There they are!" cried a gruff voice. "They're going into the cave!"

"Run!" shouted Biff.

They couldn't run back outside because the two ogres were coming, so Lee ran into one of the gloomy tunnels. He followed its twists and turns deeper and deeper under the mountain.

Finally Lee stopped. "Is that far enough, Biff?" he asked. There was no answer. "Biff?"

Oh no! When they were running, Biff must have gone down a different tunnel. Now Lee was all alone in the dark.

He wasn't alone for long. He could hear gruff voices and heavy footsteps approaching.

"Should I run?" thought Lee. "Where to?"

He looked round in a panic and saw a big rock. He ducked down behind it, just before the two ogres from outside stomped by.

"Where is that third child?" asked one ogre. "The King's making shepherd's pie tonight!"

"Oh no!" thought Lee. "They're making shepherd's pie . . . but they're using Kipper and Biff instead of shepherds!"

When the ogres had gone, Lee jumped up.

"That does it," he said to himself. "I will *not* let my friends be made into a pie!"

He set off in the direction the ogres had gone.

Finally he saw a faint glow around the next corner.
He could hear the clang of pots and pans being used.

"This must be the kitchen," Lee thought.

He tiptoed forwards.

Lee jumped out into the light of the kitchen and grabbed the nearest thing to hand. It was a frying pan. He waved this around and shouted, "Kipper! Biff! I'm here to save you!"

"Hi, Lee," said Kipper. "Where have you been?"
He was grating cheese while Biff peeled potatoes.
Lee was confused. "I thought the King of the Ogres
was cooking with *you*!" he said.

"I *am* cooking with them," piped up a little ogre with oven gloves and a crown. "It's such fun cooking with new friends!"

"Don't worry, Lee," said Biff. "We got the wrong end of the stick earlier. It was all a misunderstanding!"

Lee lowered the frying pan.

"But . . . I thought the King wanted to have us for dinner?" he said.

"Oh, I *do*!" declared the King. "I love having guests for dinner! Tonight we're having shepherd's pie!"

There was a loud cheer from the other ogres.
Shepherd's pie was their favourite.

"So . . . there are no shepherds in the shepherd's pie?"
asked Lee.

"Of course not!" said the King. "There's no meat at
all. We're strict vegetarians, you know!"

Lee realised that he was hungry too.

"It does smell delicious," he said.

When the food was ready, the three children had to stand on chairs to reach the table.

"So how did you like your first adventure?" Biff
asked Lee.

"I didn't like it at all, to begin with," answered
Lee. "I was cold and frightened and all alone . . ."

"But now I love it," Lee continued. "And all that running around has given me a *monster appetite!*"

They all began to tuck in before the key's glow told them it was time to go home.

Talk about the story

Why did the children run away when they saw the ogre?

What made Lee brave enough to try to save Biff and Kipper?

What did the king of the ogres really want?

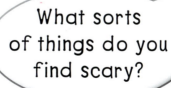

What sorts of things do you find scary?

What are the words?

Add **re** to the following to make six words with endings that make the sound /er/. Then match the words to the pictures.

theat____

lit____

spect____

cent____

og____

met____

Tips for reading *The Secret Pop Star*

Children learn best when reading is relaxed and enjoyable.

- Talk about the title and the picture on page 42.
  Then read the speech bubble.

- Discuss what you think the story might be about.

- Encourage your child to read as much of the story as they can.

- Give lots of praise as your child reads, and help them
  when necessary.

- If your child gets stuck on a word that is decodable, encourage
  them to say the sounds and then blend them together to read the
  word. Read the whole sentence again. Focus on the meaning.

- If the word is not decodable, or is still too tricky, just read the
  word for them, re-read the sentence and move on.

- Where you can, use voices for different characters. Encourage
  your child to do the same. Reading with expression is fun.

- When you've finished reading the story, talk about it with your
  child, using the 'Talk about the story' questions at the end.
  Then do the activity.

Children enjoy re-reading stories, and this helps to build
their confidence.

Have fun!

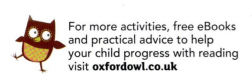

For more activities, free eBooks
and practical advice to help
your child progress with reading
visit **oxfordowl.co.uk**

The Secret Pop Star

Why is the pop star in disguise?

Wilma, Biff and Chip were watching a new music video on the computer.

"This Way Up is my favourite band ever!" said Wilma. "They're brilliant!"

"What's all this noise?" asked Dad.

"It isn't noise, Dad," said Biff. "It's the new song by This Way Up."

Dad watched the video for a moment.

"Do you call *that* dancing?" he said. "*This* is dancing!"

Dad started to do a few dance moves of his own. Biff and Chip shook their heads.

"Please stop," said Chip. "Dads can't dance!"

Later that afternoon, Mum took the children shopping in town.

There were lots of people waiting outside the concert hall.

"This Way Up is playing a concert here tonight," said Wilma.

Wilma looked sad. "My mum tried to buy tickets for us but they were sold out," she said.

They stopped and looked at a poster of the band.

"Which one do you like best?" asked Wilma.

Biff thought hard. "Alfie's the best singer, but Teddy's the best dancer," she said. "I like Teddy the best!"

While she was saying this, a man with sunglasses and a big bushy beard walked by.

Wilma turned round and stared at the man with the beard.

"What's the matter, Wilma?" asked Chip.

"That man looks very familiar . . ." said Wilma.

Suddenly the man sneezed. For just a moment, his beard slipped down.

Wilma gasped. "That beard isn't real!" she said, pointing excitedly. "I know who that man is . . . he's Teddy from This Way Up!"

"Shall we ask him for an autograph?" asked Biff.

A couple of This Way Up fans overheard Wilma.

"Did you hear what that girl just said?" one fan shouted. "It's Teddy!"

The man with the beard looked back over his shoulder. Then he started to hurry away.

More and more fans had heard the news about Teddy and were rushing over.

"Teddy!" shouted one fan. "We love you!"

The man with the fake beard broke into a run.

"Teddy!" screamed one of the fans. "Come back!"

The eager fans pushed past the children and Mum.
They started to run after the man.

"I think we'd better get home," said Mum.

As they got into the car, Wilma and Biff chatted happily about spotting the singer.

"I just hope he's OK," said Chip. "All those fans were very excited."

Before she drove off, Mum looked in the rear-view mirror.

"Um, look behind you, children," she said.

The children turned and saw someone running towards them. It was Teddy!

The pop star looked worried.

"Quick!" said Biff. "Get in!"

Teddy looked back nervously. He could see the fans running round the corner towards him.

Then he jumped in the car and Mum drove off.

Chip looked through the rear window. The fans were howling in disappointment.

Inside the car, Teddy was still out of breath from running. "Thank you," he panted.

Wilma couldn't believe Teddy was sitting right in
front of her.

"But what were you doing in that disguise?"
she asked.

Teddy grinned nervously. "It's the only way I can go
outside on my own without fans spotting me."

"Where can I drop you off?" asked Mum.

"There'll be fans outside the hotel," said Teddy. "Is it OK if I come to your house? I can call our manager from there."

"Is it OK?" said Biff. "Yes!"

At home, Teddy made a call to his manager.

When he had finished, Dad was looking at him
with a puzzled expression.

"You look familiar," he told Teddy. "You work in the
little shop on the corner, don't you?"

"Um . . ." said Teddy.

"He's a famous pop star, Dad!" said Biff.

"So maybe Floppy shouldn't be jumping all over him," said Chip. "Get down, Floppy!"

Just then the doorbell rang.

"That must be my manager," said Teddy.

Biff opened the door.

A woman thrust a microphone towards her.

"Is it true that Teddy from This Way Up is in your house?" she demanded.

Behind the woman there were lots of people with flashing cameras.

Without answering, Biff shut the door quickly.

"That wasn't your manager," she told Teddy. "There are lots of reporters outside!"

Mum went to close the curtains at the front of the house.

"There are lots of fans arriving, too!" she said.

Teddy looked worried again. "I'm really sorry about this," he said. "How am I ever going to get past that crowd?"

Wilma was grinning. "I've got an idea," she said.

Outside the crowd in the street had grown bigger and bigger. More fans joined the photographers and reporters.

Suddenly a reporter shouted, "Look! Someone's coming from the back of the house on a bike!"

The cyclist was wearing sunglasses and had a big, bushy beard.

"That's the same disguise he was wearing before!" shouted a fan. "It's Teddy!"

"After him!" shouted a photographer. The crowd began to charge after the bike.

The cyclist kept looking over his shoulder as he turned one corner and another.

Then he stopped. He was in a dead end. Slowly he got off his bike and turned to face the crowd.

"Take that silly disguise off, Teddy, and show us some dance moves!" shouted a photographer.

"OK then," said the cyclist, pulling the sunglasses and beard off.

"That's not Teddy!" yelled a fan. "That looks like someone's dad!"

Dad didn't know any dance moves by This Way Up, but he didn't want to disappoint the crowd. He decided to show them some of his own dance moves.

Meanwhile Mum and the children were driving off with Teddy in the car.

"I can hear booing," said Wilma.

"That probably means the crowd has caught up with Dad," said Chip with a grin.

Mum and the children took Teddy to meet
his manager.

"Thanks for everything," said the pop star. "I'd like
all of you to come to the concert tonight. You can be
my guests."

That evening, the whole family was excited as they
arrived for the concert. Teddy was waiting for them in
a room behind the stage.

"Come and meet the rest of the band!" he said with
a smile.

When the concert started, the family watched from the side of the stage.

Teddy spoke to the crowd. "This song is for my friends Wilma, Biff and Chip," he said.

As the song started, the band did one of their new
dance routines.

Dad watched every step and backflip very carefully.
"They're not *too* bad . . . I suppose," he said.

Talk about the story

Why is the pop star running away?

Why does Dad think Teddy looks familiar?

How did Teddy get back to his hotel?

Who are your favourite pop stars?

Escape route!

Help Teddy escape from the reporters! Find a route through the maze to the rest of the band.

Tips for reading *Fireball in the Sky*

Children learn best when reading is relaxed and enjoyable.

- Talk about the title and the picture on page 78.
  Then read the speech bubble.

- Discuss what you think the story might be about.

- Encourage your child to read as much of the story as they can.

- Give lots of praise as your child reads, and help them
  when necessary.

- If your child gets stuck on a word that is decodable, encourage
  them to say the sounds and then blend them together to read the
  word. Read the whole sentence again. Focus on the meaning.

- If the word is not decodable, or is still too tricky, just read the
  word for them, re-read the sentence and move on.

- Where you can, use voices for different characters. Encourage
  your child to do the same. Reading with expression is fun.

- When you've finished reading the story, talk about it with your
  child, using the 'Talk about the story' questions at the end.
  Then do the activity.

Children enjoy re-reading stories, and this helps to build
their confidence.

Have fun!

For more activities, free eBooks
and practical advice to help
your child progress with reading
visit **oxfordowl.co.uk**

Fireball in the Sky

Who are the aliens who arrive with the fireball, and what do they want?

On the news it said there would be lots of shooting stars that night. Nadim had come to watch in the back garden with Biff and Chip.

"Shooting stars aren't real stars," Mum explained. "They're bits of rock from space that burn up as they come close to Earth."

The children gazed up at the night sky.

"What if we saw alien spaceships instead of
shooting stars?" said Chip.

"Let's hope they'd be nice, friendly aliens!"
laughed Biff.

Nadim grinned. He loved films and books about
spaceships and aliens.

"In most science fiction stories, aliens don't just come to say hello," Nadim said. "Sometimes they come to invade Earth!"

Biff shivered. "I hope those aliens don't mind cold weather then," she said. "It's getting chilly. Let's go in and get our jackets."

When they went upstairs, Nadim noticed a glow from behind Biff's door.

"It's the magic key," he said. "I wonder where it's going to take us this time."

"We'll soon find out!" said Biff, as the magic whisked them away.

They found themselves outside under a different star-filled sky.

Chip pointed to several buildings nearby. "Look," he said. "We're on a farm."

Biff and Nadim were not looking where Chip was pointing.

"Look!" cried Nadim. "There's a shooting star!"

The children watched the shooting star as it streaked across the sky.

"That's odd," said Nadim. "It isn't burning up."

Suddenly they heard a voice behind them.
The children turned to see a big teenager shining a torch at them.

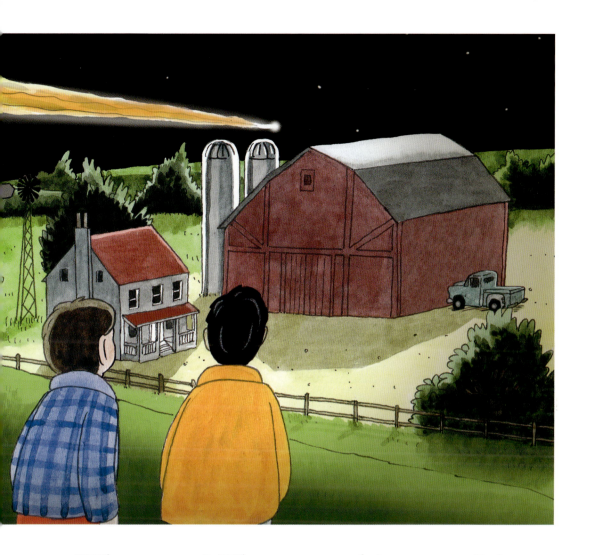

"Who are you? What are you doing on my Pa's land?" he said.

Before the children could answer him, there was a strange noise from above them.

Everybody looked up. The light in the dark sky looked like a ball of fire now.

"It's going to hit the ground!" shouted Biff.

There was a booming sound as the fireball landed
on the far side of the barn.

"Let's go and see," said Nadim.

"Wait!" The teenager held up one hand. "This is
Wilkins Farm, and *I'm* Hank Wilkins. I'm going first."

Hank set off and the children followed him.

When they reached the field, they gasped.
A perfectly round object sat in the middle of a hole in
the ground. Smoke was rising from it.

"That isn't a bit of rock," said Biff. "Look. It's
smooth and silver."

"This is just like a science fiction film!" said Nadim.

Suddenly there was a hissing sound and a door
appeared in the side of the silver ball.

The children watched in amazement as a strange
little creature flopped out on to the ground.

Hank stepped forward and said, "What are *you*
doing on my Pa's land?"

The strange creature looked at them with huge eyes and clasped its bony hands together.

"Please, help me!" it said. "My name is Mendax and I'm in terrible, terrible danger. You must hide me before they come and find me!"

"Before *who* come and find you?" demanded Hank.

Mendax pointed a long, trembling finger up to the skies.

The children looked up and saw a much bigger light approaching.

"Please help!" repeated Mendax. "The Grozzers are chasing me. Hide me! *Please!*"

After a few seconds' thought, Hank nodded slowly. "Pa's truck is over near the barn," he said. "We can hide behind that."

As they ran, a strange humming sound came from the sky. It got louder and louder.

"Their spaceship's going to land!" wailed Mendax.

As the children hid, a huge, disc-shaped object hovered in the sky. It landed next to the crater that Mendax's ship had made.

"The Grozzers have been after me for days," Mendax whispered. "They're very dangerous!"

A door in the Grozzers' ship opened and several new aliens marched out. These were much bigger and scarier than Mendax.

One of them started looking at Mendax's little spaceship.

"I don't like the look of this," said Nadim quietly.

Mendax trembled. "Is there a town nearby?"
he asked. "The Grozzers won't be able to find me in a
busy place like that."

"The town's just down the road," said Hank,
pointing. "But I'm not sure you'll get there before they
catch you."

Mendax smiled broadly, showing his sharp little teeth. "I might be able to get away if you can distract them," he said.

"Won't that be dangerous?" asked Hank.

Mendax shook his head. "The Grozzers don't care about you. They only want to catch me."

Biff nodded bravely. "You three do your best
to distract the Grozzers," she said. "I'll take Mendax
as far as the main road into town. I'll be back in
ten minutes."

She ran off with Mendax towards the road.

Chip and Nadim glanced towards the Grozzers' ship. The aliens were starting to search the area.

"We need a brilliant idea to distract them," said Chip.

Hank ran forwards, waving his arms around and shouting, "Hey! Over here!" at the top of his voice.

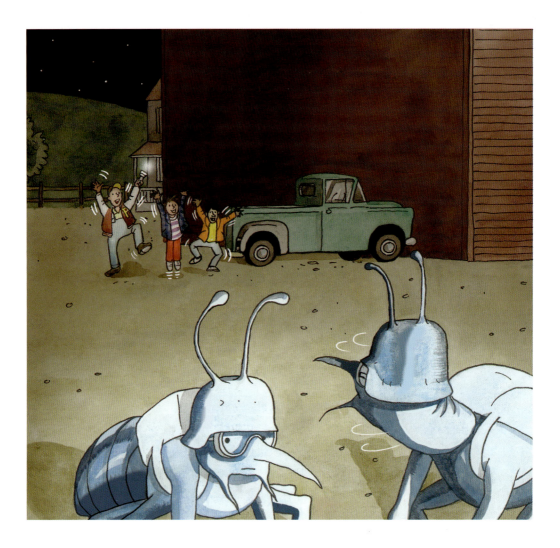

There was nothing Chip and Nadim could do except follow Hank and join in.

"This way, Grozzers!" shouted Nadim.

"Come and get us!" shouted Chip.

Moments later a few of the Grozzers zipped up to them on scooters that hovered just above the ground.

The first Grozzer lifted its goggles and fixed the boys with blazing eyes. "Where can we find Mendax?" it demanded. "Tell us."

"He's gone," said Nadim firmly. "You've missed him and now you'll never catch him."

The Grozzers looked suddenly worried. "That's terrible," the second one said. "Once Mendax has learned all about your world, he will send a report to his home planet. Then his people will invade your little world."

Nadim was shocked. "You mean, *Mendax* wants to take over planet Earth?"

"Quick!" said Chip. "Mendax is on his way to the town, and my sister Biff is with him!"

"We must stop him!" said the Grozzers. "Mendax can change his appearance to look like any other living creature. If he reaches town, we'll lose him forever. Let's go!"

Biff was close to the main road now, but she slowed down when she heard a strange noise behind her.

She turned round and gasped. Mendax was not there. Instead, an exact copy of Biff herself was staring back at her.

"What's going on?" asked Biff.

"Silence, Earth child!" commanded the Biff lookalike with a nasty grin.

"Is that you, Mendax?" asked Biff.

"Of course!" answered the copy of Biff. "Even if the Grozzers catch us, they'll arrest *you*, not *me*! Nothing will stop my people from taking over Earth!"

Moments later the Grozzers zoomed up on their hover-scooters. The two Biffs turned to meet them.

"Which one is Mendax?" demanded one Grozzer.

"That's Mendax!" said one Biff, pointing angrily.

"No!" said the other Biff, also pointing.

"*That's* Mendax!"

The first Grozzer turned to his companion. He whispered, "We must ask something that only an Earth person would get right."

The second Grozzer nodded, then said, "How did you arrive at this place?"

"I came on my bike," said one Biff quickly.

"That's not true," said the other Biff. "Mendax landed in a spaceship. And I . . . well, a magic key brought me here."

The Grozzers looked at each other. "Our files say bikes are a common form of transport here," said one. "We have no record of 'magic keys'."

A Grozzer turned to the real Biff. "Come with us, Mendax," it said. "We're taking you home."

"Wait!" shouted a voice behind them. "There really is a magic key!"

Chip was running down the lane as fast as he could. Nadim and Hank were not far behind.

Once the boys arrived, Mendax knew that his chance to escape was over. With a shimmer of light, he returned to his normal form.

Mendax screwed up his nose as he looked around. "I'm not sure I even want to invade this place any more," he sniffed.

They went back to the Grozzer ship.

"Mendax is safely on board," explained one Grozzer. "Thanks for your help, Earth children."

"Will you visit our planet again?" asked Nadim.

"Perhaps," said the second Grozzer. "When you humans are ready for it . . ."

The children watched as the Grozzers' ship took off,
then whooshed away into the night.

In Chip's hand the magic key began glowing.

Before they left, they heard a shout from the
farmhouse. "Hank! What's going on out there?"

Hank winked at the children. "Nothing, Pa. Go
back to sleep!"

Talk about the story

What are shooting stars?

How did Mendax persuade the children to help him?

How did the Grozzers try to work out who was the real Biff?

What do you think about spaceships and aliens?

Odd one out

Add *-ball* to these words to make five compound words.
For example, fire + ball = fireball.

basket   cannon   eye   foot   snow

Match the pictures to the new words. Which picture is the
odd one out?

Tips for reading *A Knight in Town*

Children learn best when reading is relaxed and enjoyable.

- Talk about the title and the picture on page 114.
  Then read the speech bubble.

- Discuss what you think the story might be about.

- Encourage your child to read as much of the story as they can.

- Give lots of praise as your child reads, and help them
  when necessary.

- If your child gets stuck on a word that is decodable, encourage
  them to say the sounds and then blend them together to read the
  word. Read the whole sentence again. Focus on the meaning.

- If the word is not decodable, or is still too tricky, just read the
  word for them, re-read the sentence and move on.

- Where you can, use voices for different characters. Encourage
  your child to do the same. Reading with expression is fun.

- When you've finished reading the story, talk about it with your
  child, using the 'Talk about the story' questions at the end.
  Then do the activity.

Children enjoy re-reading stories, and this helps to build
their confidence.

Have fun!

For more activities, free eBooks
and practical advice to help
your child progress with reading
visit **oxfordowl.co.uk**

A Knight in Town

What happens to the knight in town?

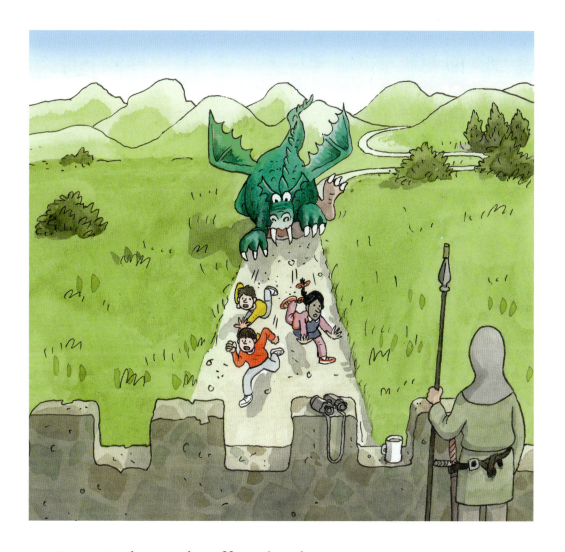

"Run!" shouted Biff. "The dragon's coming this way!"

Biff, Chip and Anneena were on an adventure. The magic key had brought them to a land where there were dragons.

The children sprinted towards the castle. Behind them a huge dragon roared and raged.

They reached the castle just in time. They charged
through the great wooden door and some men quickly
pushed it shut. The children heard the roar of the
dragon from the other side.

"This door will keep any dragon out," grunted one
of the gatekeepers.

"I don't think so," said Anneena. "It's a wooden door and dragons breathe fire!"

"Oh," said the man. "I didn't think of that."

"There haven't been any dragons here for years," explained another gatekeeper. "Usually they stay far off in the mountains."

The children heard a clanking sound behind them. A group of knights in armour were walking towards the door.

The biggest knight held his helmet under one arm. "You can leave the dragon to us now," he told the gatekeepers.

"What are you going to do?" asked Chip.

The big knight glanced down at the three children. "Battle the dragon, of course," he boomed. "That's what knights do."

"Percy's not afraid of anything," said one of the others, pointing at the big knight.

Anneena looked worried. "The dragon's scary, but I hope the knights won't hurt it," she said. "I don't want to see that."

"Don't worry," said Biff. "Look."

The magic key was glowing in her hand.

"But the adventure isn't over yet!" Chip exclaimed.

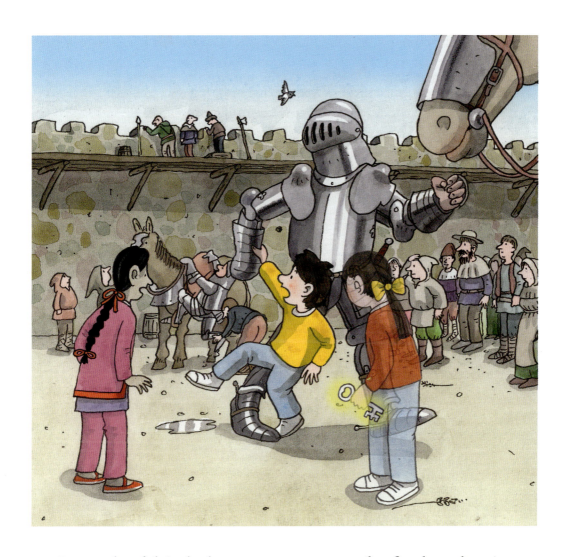

Percy had his helmet on now, ready for battle. As he walked towards his horse, he bumped into Chip. To stop himself from falling, Chip reached out and grabbed Percy's arm.

At that moment, the magic whisked the children home.

"We're back home before the end of the adventure,"
complained Chip. "That doesn't usually happen!"

"There's something else unusual, too," said Anneena.

Biff and Chip turned and saw a big suit of armour.
Then the armour moved!

Percy lifted his helmet off and stared down at the children. "What strange magic is this?" he demanded. He looked around. "And what is this nightmarish place?"

Biff was shocked. All she could say was, "Erm . . . it's my bedroom."

Downstairs, Kipper was making cookies with Gran.
Mum and Dad were away and so Gran was looking
after the children.

Chip came to the kitchen door. "Gran, can you help
us, please?"

Gran saw how worried Chip was. "Is everything
OK?" she asked.

Before Chip could answer, Percy appeared behind him.

"A knight!" cried Kipper in surprise.

Percy bowed towards Gran. Then he asked, "Are you the ruler of this strange land?"

Gran was just as surprised as Kipper, but she hid it well. "Yes," she said. "I am."

Gran led everyone into the living room.

"Sit there," she told Percy, "and don't let your armour rip the sofa, please." She turned to the children. "Now tell me exactly what happened."

When they had finished, Gran scratched her head. "You're right," she said. "This is *very* unusual."

Suddenly the oven timer peeped in the kitchen. Percy leaped up, ready for battle.

"Sit back down," Gran told him. "That sound just means the cookies are ready to eat." She went to the door. "Biff and Chip, can you come and help me, please?"

In the kitchen, Gran whispered, "It's very important that we don't let anyone else see Percy. What would people think of a real knight in armour? We'll just have to keep him here until the key glows again."

Anneena and Kipper were not sure what to say to
Percy. The knight sat silently on the sofa.

"Let's watch television," suggested Kipper, clicking
the remote control.

When he saw the television, Percy's eyes opened
wide in shock. "Who trapped those tiny people in your
magic mirror?" he demanded.

"I'll just turn the television off," said Kipper quickly.

Percy jumped up. "Enough!" he shouted. "I've had enough of this terrible place and its strange magic! I must go back to where I belong. I'll battle any army to find my way home. I'll slay any dragon!"

"There aren't any dragons here," said Anneena kindly.

Just then a loud rumble from outside made the windows shake. A big truck drove past with a yellow digger on the back.

"A dragon!" shouted Percy. He clanked towards the front door.

When Biff, Chip and Gran heard all the shouting, they came running.

"Where's Percy?" asked Chip.

"He's gone," said Kipper.

"He ran outside," added Anneena. "He went chasing after a digger. He thinks it's a dragon!"

They all hurried to the front door.

There was no sign of Percy on the street.

"We'd better catch up with him before he gets into any trouble," said Gran.

"I bet that digger was going to the town centre," said Chip. "They're building a new library there."

The children and Gran set off.

Round the corner they saw a man in a bike helmet.

"Excuse me," said Biff. "Have you seen a knight in armour?"

"Yes," said the cyclist crossly. "He watched me ride up on my bike. Then, when I stopped, he grabbed it and rode off on it!"

Gran and the children hurried on, until at last they saw the building site.

"Look," said Chip, pointing. "The workers are unloading the digger from the back of the truck. But I can't see Percy anywhere. Where is he?"

Suddenly a loud voice from across the road boomed,
"Get ready to meet your doom, foul beast!"

Percy was sitting on the bike and staring right at
the digger. In one hand he waved a colourful umbrella.

"That's *our* umbrella!" said Chip.

Percy set off towards the digger, holding the umbrella out like a sword. He wobbled a bit at first, but soon he was going faster and faster.

The children waved their arms.

"Stop!" shouted Biff. "That *isn't* a dragon!"

Percy had not learned how to use the brakes. When
he saw the children, he swerved the bike away from
them and bumped right into the kerb.

"Be careful!" shouted Chip, but it was too late.
Percy landed with a loud clang.

Percy sat with his head in his hands. "I just want to go home," he said glumly.

"I think you're in luck then," said Anneena with a smile. "Show him, Biff."

Biff held up the magic key, which had begun to glow faintly again.

On the way home, Gran made sure that Percy took the bike back and said sorry. By the time they reached the house, the magic key was glowing brighter.

"What now?" asked Percy.

The children led him back to Biff's room.

"It's time for you to go home!" said Biff.

The magic did take Percy back to his world, and it took Biff, Chip and Anneena there again, too.

Percy was glad to be back. The other knights came running up to him.

"Where've you been, Percy?" asked one. "We have to slay that dragon right now!"

"No," said Anneena firmly. "There has to be another way."

"Don't be silly!" began one of the knights.

Anneena went on. "That dragon's a long way from home. It must be lost and confused." She glanced at Percy. "You know how that feels, don't you?"

Percy nodded, remembering his own adventure.

"But we have to slay the dragon," said the other knight. "That's what knights do!"

Percy shook his head. "That's not true. We do the *right* thing."

At that moment Chip and Biff spotted something in the sky.

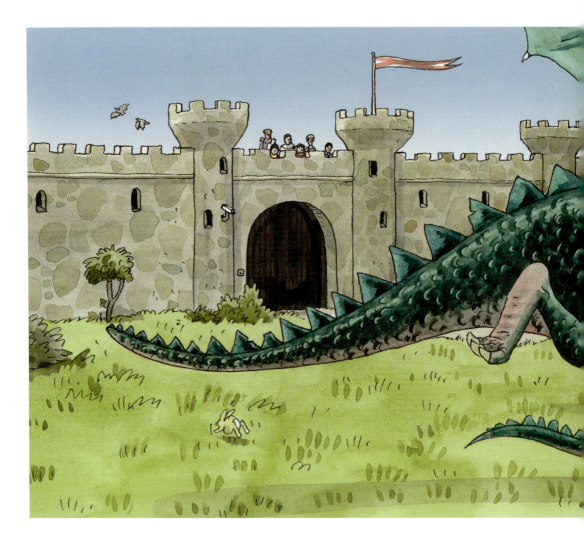

A second, *much* bigger dragon was swooping down.

"Maybe it's the other dragon's parent!"
said Anneena.

This dragon looked big enough to crush the castle
walls with its claws. One flick of its tail could smash
the castle's turrets to rubble.

But the new dragon left the castle alone. It swooped low and gently scooped up the smaller dragon with its front legs.

Then, flapping its huge wings, it turned round and began to fly home towards the mountains.

Anneena watched until the dragons were no more than a dot in the distance.

"Now the adventure's *really* over," said Chip. "I bet we'll go home soon."

Percy smiled. "Perhaps one day I too will return to your land. I'd like to see Queen Gran again and try the mysterious food known as cookies."

Talk about the story

How does the knight end up in the children's house?

Why does the knight think that the digger is a dragon?

How does Anneena help to save the dragon from being slain by the knights?

Where would you like to go on an imaginary adventure?

What's the word?

Use the clues to work out the words that begin with *kn-*. For example, a soldier in the past who held high rank = knight.

to make a garment from wool using two needles

to make a sound by tapping on wood

a round lump or ball (like a door handle)

understanding and remembering information

the result of tying two ends of string together

a sharp blade for cutting things

the joint between your thigh and lower leg

the joints where your fingers join your hands

Remembering the stories together

Encourage your child to remember and retell the stories in this book.
You could ask questions like these:

- Who are the characters?
- What happens at the beginning?
- What happens next?

- How does the story end?
- What was your favourite part? Why?

Story prompts

When talking to your child about the stories, you could use these more detailed reminders to help them remember the exact sequence of events. Turn the statements below into questions, so that your child can give you the answers. For example, *Who is staying at Kipper's house? What are they reading about?* And so on …

The Ogre's Dinner

- Lee is staying at Kipper's house.
- They are reading a book about ogres when the magic key takes them to a dark forest. Suddenly an ogre appears!
- The King of the Ogres invites the children to dinner, but they think that they are going to be eaten.

- Biff and Lee are chased by two ogres as they try to find Kipper.
- Lee finds Biff and Kipper in the kitchen helping the King.
- They all have a great feast.

The Secret Popstar

- The family are in town with Mum and find out that *This Way Up* is playing a concert there that night.
- Wilma spots Teddy from the band. Some fans start to run after Teddy, so the family help him escape.

- Teddy comes to their house and reporters surround the house.
- They help Teddy escape again and he gives them all tickets to the show as a thank you.

Fireball in the Sky

- The children are hoping to see shooting stars when the magic key takes them on an adventure.

- Suddenly there is a booming sound and a strange creature comes out of a silver ball asking for help to hide from the Grozzers.

- The Grozzers tell the children that Mendax wants to take over planet Earth.

- Mendax changes his appearance to look like Biff.

- Chip saves Biff by confirming to the Grozzers that there is a magic key as real Biff says!

- Mendax is taken onto the spaceship by the Grozzers.

A Knight in Town

- The magic key takes Biff, Chip and Anneena to a land full of dragons.

- They are chased to a castle by a dragon, and then inside the castle a group of knights surround them.

- The magic key whisks the children home along with Percy, a knight.

- Percy is confused and chases after a digger that he thinks is a dragon.

- Gran and the children run after Percy and find him having an umbrella fight with the digger at a building site!

- The children rescue Percy and the magic key manages to take him back home where he has learned his lesson.

You could now encourage your child to create a 'story map' of each story, drawing and colouring all the key parts of them. This will help them to identify the main elements of the stories and learn to create their own stories.